Teaching Preschoolers:
It Looks Like This...
In Pictures

Jeannette G. Stone

A 1990-91 Comprehensive Membership benefit

National Association for the Education of Young Children
Washington, DC 20009-5786

National Association for the Education of Young Children
1834 Connecticut Avenue, N.W.
Washington, DC 20009-5786

The National Association for the Education of Young Children attempts through its publications program to provide a forum for discussion of major issues and ideas in our field. We hope to provoke thought and promote professional growth. The views expressed or implied are not necessarily those of the Association.

Library of Congress Catalog Card Number: 90-62661

ISBN Catalog Number: 0-935989-38-2

NAEYC #: 305

Book design: Jeannette G. Stone and Jack Zibulsky; Cover design: Polly Greenberg and Jeannette G. Stone; Production: Jack Zibulsky

Printed in the United States of America.

In appreciation

I want to thank the people who made this book possible. They gave of themselves with the kind of energy and selflessness for which early childhood educators are known.

I thank Polly Greenberg of NAEYC for her encouragement and dedication to quality as she discussed with me, along the way, my pictures and text. She reviewed the book with generous and sensitive consideration of my intent.

My thanks, too, to the other reviewers:

Margaret Copeland, Colby-Sawyer College, New London, New Hampshire

Jenni Klein, Bethesda, Maryland

Dorothy Shellow, Bethesda, Maryland

Docia Zavitkovsky, Los Angeles, California.

To all of the children and families, staff members, and administrators who participated, I am deeply appreciative. I owe debts of gratitude especially to Judy Hanf, Director of the Leila Day Nursery, Inc., a fine day care center in New Haven, Connecticut; and to Mary Eisenberg, former Leila Day Nursery Director (now Director of the Lotus Children's Center in Cambridge, Massachusetts).

At the Leila Day Nursery, teachers Susan MacDonald and Rose Giles Jones offered me unlimited opportunities, over a year, to study and photograph all that went on in their classroom. Other Leila Day staff members also welcomed me with my camera in the interests of capturing in pictures the typical happenings in preschool education.

* * * * * * * * * * * * * * * *

In dedication

Jenni Klein contributed in special ways. She gave consideration to each picture and paragraph, responding with thoughtful candor and with her comprehensive knowledge of the field. I dedicate this book to Jenni in appreciation for her loyal support now and over the many years we have been friends and colleagues.

Jeannette G. Stone

Fall, 1990

A note to the reader...

"A picture is worth a thousand words," the saying goes. The idea for this book developed from the growing belief that educational theories come to life when we see them in actual practice. For example, when we discuss "quality education" or "developmentally appropriate practice," it helps to visualize what we are saying.

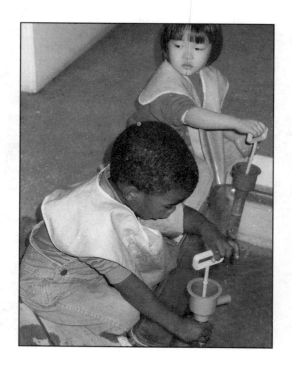

What is the look of a quality preschool program? Some might think of it as akin to kindergarten or first grade with structured language, math, and art projects. Others would argue for children's need to play with good materials of their own choice in a program geared for exploration and interaction. Many would recommend a balance of child-initiated and teacher-initiated activities.

On these pages you will see developmental programs as they progress through the day—parents and children arriving, meals and snacks, group meeting, children's activities in and out of doors, cleanup, and so forth. How do teachers set up their programs? Are materials prepared ahead of time? Then: What do teachers do while children play? Can they guide their play without intruding? How does appropriate discipline look (discipline more effective and fair than repeated time-out or punishment)? Does it look like re-direction? Explanation? Listening and problem solving? How do teachers help children transform strong feelings and aggression into language and cooperative play?

Consider the issue of free play when children choose their own activities and pursue their own interests: There is a big difference between free play that looks aimless or even wild and free play that looks absorbing, educational, and orderly. Is it the teacher who makes this difference? How important are curriculum, scheduling, room arrangement?

Teachers have successful and not-so-great days, but they want always to be good with children. This book is designed to help by showing pictures of children and competent teachers living through typical, unposed hours of day care, nursery school, Head Start, and kindergarten. You, the reader, are asked to examine the pictures and to study them critically. Do the pictures mirror your experiences and philosophy? How do you react to the teaching you see on these pages? These pictures of real preschool life may help as you reflect on how you want to approach your own work with young children.

Note about text and quotations

Quotations throughout this book, at the bottom of pages, come from three sources:

1. Developmentally Appropriate Practice in Early Childhood Programs Serving Children From Birth Through Age 8. Sue Bredekamp, Editor, NAEYC, 1987.
2. Curriculum Planning for Young Children. Janet F. Brown, Editor, NAEYC, 1982.
3. Accreditation Criteria & Procedures of the National Academy of Early Childhood Programs. Sue Bredekamp, Editor, NAEYC, 1987.

Page numbers accompany each quotation, along with a reference to "DAP" or "Curriculum Planning" or "Accreditation." The rest of the text, incorporated with the pictures, is my own.

Note about photographs

This book shows the children's programs that I visited and photographed during the year when this book was undergoing intensive preparation. (Two pictures date back to the 1970s.)
- Calvin Hill Day Care Center, and the Kitty Lustman-Findling Kindergarten, New Haven, Connecticut
- Concord Hospital Day Care Center, Concord, New Hampshire
- Cold Spring School, New Haven, Connecticut
- Early Childhood Center, Sarah Lawrence College, Bronxville, New York
- Eastchester Child Development Center and Head Start Child Care, Tuckahoe, New York
- Leila Day Nursery, New Haven, Connecticut
- Montessori Children's Center, Littleton, New Hampshire
- Poughkeepsie Family Development and Day Care Center, Poughkeepsie, New York
- Project Head Start centers, New Haven, Connecticut

These programs provide open enrollment to include children of all economic, educational, ethnic, racial, and religious backgrounds. Five include kindergarten classrooms.

About the author

Jeannette Galambos Stone retired in 1982 from Sarah Lawrence College where she taught Early Childhood Education and directed the Early Childhood Center laboratory school. Unable to cease her involvement, she has served since retirement as a consultant in day care centers, Head Start, CDA, and in nursery schools in Connecticut, Massachusetts, and New Hampshire. Jeannette has written about children and teaching throughout her career, authoring <u>A Guide to Discipline</u> and, more recently, <u>Teacher-Parent Relationships</u> for NAEYC.

Jeannette began teaching in 1953, working in cooperative nursery schools first and then in Head Start and day care programs—teaching in the classroom and then administering children's centers as well as developing teacher-training programs for staff and for student-teachers.

Jeannette graduated from Oberlin College in 1939 with a Music major and earned an M.Ed. from the University of Maryland in 1964. She credits her colleague, Jenni Klein, and her professor, Jimmy Hymes, for their major contributions to her progress.

During the 1960s and 70s, Jeannette helped produce educational films for Head Start and for the Institute for Child Mental Health, as a member of the Vassar College Child Development Film Program; and she has observed child care practices in Israel, Europe, and the Far East.

She currently teaches Early Childhood Education at the New Hampshire Technical Institute in Concord, New Hampshire, where she lives, and spends as much time as possible with her grown daughters and her grandchildren.

Table of contents

Section 1. Characteristics of good teachers..1

Section 2. As the days begin..2
        parents are welcome..3
        saying goodbye...4

Section 3. Breakfast (or early snack)..5

Section 4. Group meeting time..6

Section 5. Music..7
        Story..8

Section 6. Transition...9

Section 7. Room set-up
        organizing the play environment...10
        blocks..11
        "house"...12
        other learning centers and manipulatives..13
        water and sand...14
        art materials..15

Section 8. During play time
        art activities..16
        at the easel...17
        other activities...18
        other materials...19
        sand and water...20-21
        informal activities in the kindergarten...22
        moving from one activity to another..23
        playing "house"..24-25
        building with blocks...26-27

Section 9. Teachers alert to children's appearance, behavior....................28-29
        Observing and recording..30-31

Section 10. Discipline...32-39

Section 11. Language in a print-rich environment.....................................40-43

Table of contents

Section 12. Out of doors—more communication..44
Outdoor curriculum...45-46
Transition to indoors...47

Section 13. Self-help and adult help during routines........................48-49

Section 14. Lunch..50-51

Section 15. Cleanup—time for nap..52

Section 16. During nap..53
After nap...54-56

Section 17. Late in the afternoon...57
Early evening..58

Section 18. Conclusion..59-61

For further reading..62

Information about NAEYC...63

Section 1. Characteristics of good teachers

These children seem trusting and relaxed;
they learn from teachers who are:
 . . . warm, understanding (rather than critical)
 . . . tuned in (rather than distracted)
 . . . fair (rather than tough)
 . . . genuine (rather than over-sweet or "teachery")
 . . . good-humored (rather than irritable)
 . . . good listeners

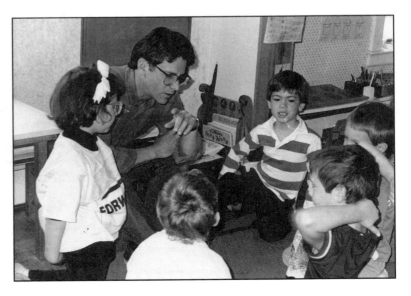

Section 2. As the days begin

A home away from home for children and their families....

"Children and their parents are greeted warmly and with enthusiasm each morning. The day begins with a great deal of adult-child contact." DAP, p. 41

Section 2. As the days begin—parents are welcome

Shawn needs a slow beginning....

Maria's mother often reads to her in the playroom before going off to work.

Another day: A father takes a few minutes to paint with his daughter.

The teachers try not to rush parents' leave-taking. Indeed, parent-teacher relationships deepen in the children's classrooms.

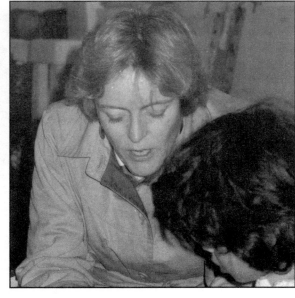

"Parents are welcome visitors in the center at all times (for example, to observe, eat lunch with a child, or volunteer to help in the classroom). Parents and other family members are encouraged to be involved in the program in various ways, taking into consideration working parents and those with little spare time." Accreditation, p. 16

Section 2. As the days begin—saying goodbye

Every morning the teacher pushes a bench under the hall window so that children can wave goodbye to mothers and fathers leaving from the parking lot. This ritual helps the children feel ready to settle into the morning's routines.

"Young children are integrally connected to their families. Programs cannot adequately meet the needs of children unless they also recognize the importance of the child's family and develop strategies to work effectively with families. All communication between centers and families should be based on the concept that parents are and should be the principal influence in children's lives." Accreditation, p. 15

Section 3. Breakfast (or early snack)

Breakfast is more than nutrition and filling empty stomachs. It's a great time for teachers and children to listen to each other and to feel a sense of shared companionship.

Suggestions for mealtimes:
1. Have 2 or 3 children clean table-tops with damp, soapy sponges.
2. Encourage children to take turns setting the table.
3. Teachers sit down, always, with the children.
4. Keep one of those sponges on the table—handy for spills.

"Children's communication skills develop from verbal interaction with adults." Accreditation, p. 9

"Adults encourage children's developing language by speaking clearly and frequently to individual children and listening to their response. Adults respond quickly and appropriately to children's verbal initiatives." DAP, p. 49

Section 4. Group meeting time

For those children who finish eating first, there is a designated spot (in this case, puzzles set out on a rug) so that the children and one of the teachers can wait together for the others. This gently directed transition allows the children to stay focused rather than wandering or getting into trouble.

Next, meeting time for group conversation begins. Occasionally the teacher brings up the calendar or weather. However, daily calendar and weather may become repetitive and boring and may lead to difficulties. Encourage the children to talk more about what is on their minds—the new baby, for example, or a grandparent's illness, or yesterday's bus ride, or a beloved television program, or a new child who will appear at the center the next day....The teacher sometimes talks about her interests, too.

Perhaps rather than Show-and-Tell....Think-and-Tell, or Remember-and-Tell.

"From infancy through the primary grades, adult communication with children is facilitated by sitting low or kneeling, making eye contact." DAP, p. 10

6

Section 5. Music

Now, while the children are gathered together (or later in the day) comes music:

> singing
>> finger plays
>>> dancing to a tape
>>>> or record...
>>>>> of Mozart
>>>>> or jazz
>>>>> or reggae
>>>>> or a folksong

"Children like to sing; they like to play musical instruments; they like to listen to records. Teachers of young children generally include musical activities daily for the pleasure they give, for the release from tension they can often provide, and for aid in developing cognitive skills...." Curriculum Planning, p. 187

Section 5. Story

In addition to informal story-reading throughout the day to individual children and to small groups, a daily scheduled story-time is planned by teachers and anticipated by children.

This teacher has chosen a book to read, in advance, and has familiarized herself with it. She doesn't merely read <u>at</u> the children; she gets involved, and she thinks about it with them.

Without allowing too much interruption, she doesn't silence the children during her reading but responds as well as she can while maintaining the momentum of the story.

" I will turn the book so you can see the pictures better, Tommy."

"<u>Think</u> about what is happening to the puppy!"

"Yes, Akiko, I'll read it again."

"Throughout early childhood, children's concepts and language gradually develop to enable them to understand...abstract or symbolic information. Pictures and stories should be used frequently to build upon children's real experiences." DAP, p. 4

Section 6. Transition

Transitions: how to move from one activity or area to another smoothly, without tumult or confusion....

At the end of group meeting, before the children disperse, the teacher leads into the transition. "It's play time next....Now is the time for you to think about what you want to do first. The easel is set up...the water table...blocks...and the 'house' corner. Mrs. B can use four helpers to make muffins over at the corner table." The teacher gives the children a minute to think about their options. She may add an idea. "Rudi and Mariko, remember you said yesterday you wanted to try that hard puzzle again?" The children proceed to choose their activities. They move from their first choice to several others in the course of the hour or two allotted to the play period.

Teacher: "Have you all seen the new little door for block-building?"

"The word __teach__ tends to imply __telling__ or __giving information__. But the correct way to teach young children is not to lecture or verbally instruct them. Teachers of young children are more like guides or facilitators. They prepare the environment so that it provides stimulating, challenging materials and activities for children." DAP, p. 52

Section 7. Room set-up—organizing the play environment

Set-up: The play areas and materials have been prepared in advance.

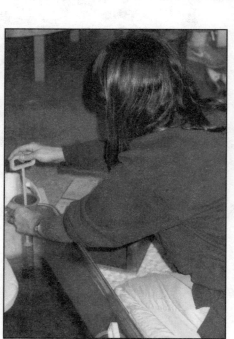

"Teachers prepare the environment for children to learn through active exploration and interaction with adults, other children, and materials. Children select many of their own activities from among a variety of learning areas the teacher prepares...." DAP, p. 54

Section 7. Room set-up—blocks

Unit Blocks: Many teachers believe that blocks are basic to a quality curriculum and are to be available every day. Plenty of blocks—stacked by shape—are unsurpassed as tools for creative construction and for trial-and-error learning about design, balance, and cooperative play. Children share ideas, efforts, and enthusiasm. Math and language concepts are embedded in unit blocks as children learn to recognize shapes, dimensions, quantities and to discover construction principles.

The benefit of working with blocks continues as a teacher helps the children re-stack them by shape at cleanup time.

Blocks can be used without added toys, but good accessories or "props" serve to refresh the scene and intensify the children's involvement over the months. Small traffic signs or miniature people and animals work well, as do cardboard tubes, little cars and trucks....These and many other props can be rotated and gradually added to over the months as the children develop more complex ideas.

"Adults provide plenty of materials and time for children to explore and learn about the environment, to exercise their natural curiosity, and to experiment with cause and effect relationships. For example, they provide blocks...." DAP, p. 49

Section 7. Room set-up—"house"

Besides blocks, what other areas are crucial to a rich play environment?

A "house" for re-enacting family life has deep and important meaning for young children from toddlerhood through primary years...

Props include a few carefully organized dress-ups, dolls dressed for the day, and household objects arranged in new and engaging ways from day to day.

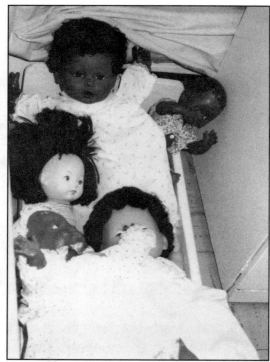

"Housekeeping, a form of dramatic play, provides social education through role playing, imitation of adults, and opportunities to play out home relationships and life experiences." Curriculum Planning, p. 28

Section 7. Room set-up—other learning centers and manipulatives

On many days the teachers' set-up includes simple math games (some home-made), or a science exhibit for hands-on play. Today some corn and squash are placed on a small table for one or two children at a time to touch, look at, wonder about, discuss.

Each day the children find a table set up with manipulatives. It looks inviting and challenging to the children if it is prepared artfully, colorfully, and if the materials change from day to day according to the children's reactions and growing abilities.

"Teachers have long been convinced that providing children with three-dimensional objects to manipulate will enhance their interest and curiosity...." Curriculum Planning, p. 126

13

Section 7. Room set-up—water and sand

An indoor "sandbox" for one works well for a particular child on a particular day, or when space is tight.

Water and sand: Some teachers set one or both of these out every day; some, every week. The water table (or water in small basins) can be fitted out with various accessories, to be rotated from time to time: pumps, small dolls, funnels, sponges, corks, an eggbeater, a kitchen syringe, measuring cups and spoons....

Having a fine supply of water-play props doesn't mean putting them all out at once! Here is a water table crowded with too many unrelated water props. Some might be saved for another day. Some might be available at a table or shelf off to the side. Clutter makes for more clutter.

"Children need to manipulate tools as part of their early childhood curriculum. A water table with sponges, funnels, straws, and squeeze bottles is essential. Likewise, a sand table with sieves, strainers, containers of various sizes and shapes, sticks, shovels, and pails gives children opportunities to use tools."
Curriculum Planning, p. 111

Section 7. Room set-up—art materials

For a teacher's idea—which any child who wishes to can try—there are table paints set out along with narrow paper strips. It looks different and interesting.

For children's own choices and ideas, there are art materials available on low, open shelves—an everyday feature of the set-up, with new materials added (and old ones temporarily removed) every few days.

"Staff provide materials and time for children to select their own activities during the day. Children may choose from among several activities which the teacher has planned or the children initiate." Accreditation, p. 13

15

Section 8. During play time—art activities

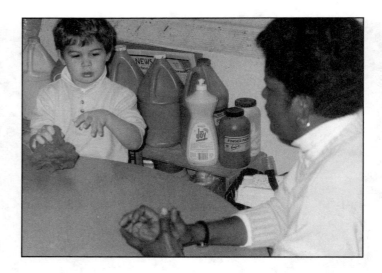

Many children choose art activities—drawing and painting with markers or cotton swabs—alone or with a friend or a teacher. Clay or playdough are available almost always.

"...measure sand, water, or ingredients for cooking; observe changes in the environment; work with wood and tools, sort objects for a purpose; explore...water, wheels and gears;...and draw, paint, and work with clay." DAP, p. 56

Section 8. During play time—at the easel

Miguel and Lori, in kindergarten, have chosen to start at the easel. They're clearly serious about their work.

"Children have daily opportunities for aesthetic expression and appreciation through art and music....A variety of art media are available for creative expression, such as easel and finger painting and clay." DAP, p. 56

Section 8. During play time—other activities

In this center there is much to do that is compelling and thought-provoking. Special-needs children are included—on the basis of sensitive and sensible intake.

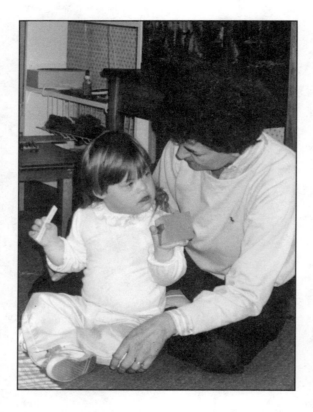

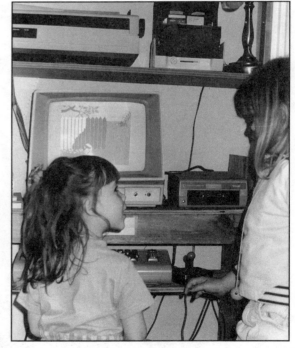

"Children acquire knowledge about the physical and social worlds in which they live through playful interaction with objects and people. Children do not need to be forced to learn; they are motivated by their own desire to make sense of their world." DAP, p. 52

Section 8. During play time—other materials

Children become engrossed in their play if the materials "grab" them—Montessori materials or computers or old familiar construction sets.

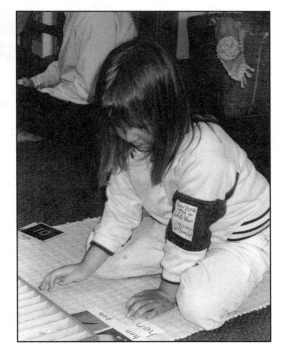

When materials are presented in careful order, children's work is more careful and orderly.

"The younger the child, the more activity should be child-initiated and individual or small group. The amount of time spent in staff-initiated, large-group activity should be minimized for all children younger than six." Accreditation, p. 12

19

Section 8. During play time—sand and water

Sand and water are natural favorites; children seem both relaxed and intent with them. They become investigators and experimenters.

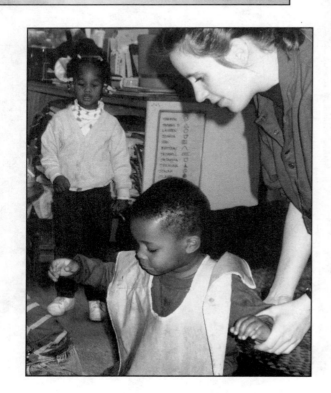

"An early childhood science program should be child-centered and activity-oriented; it should provide children with a varied environment to explore at their own pace and according to their individual cognitive abilities." Curriculum Planning, p. 149

Section 8. During play time—sand and water

Children need plenty of time to carry out their ideas. This sort of exploratory activity, to be worthwhile, takes more than a few minutes; rather, it can take an hour or more for children to examine the properties of water, to construct a block building, to paint, to pretend to be father in the house corner, then to return to the water table....

"Although young children might be limited conceptually, there are no limits, unless adults set them, to children's curiosity, imagination, zest for learning, and interest in the many things about them." Curriculum Planning, p. 146

Section 8. During play time—informal activities in the kindergarten

Kindergartners are busy during their work/play period with weaving in one corner of the room and a language arts game in another. Their teacher has chosen a hands-on, activity-centered approach to standard academic expectations for fives.

"The primary grades...curriculum is integrated so that learning occurs primarily through projects, learning centers, and playful activities that reflect current interests of children." DAP, p. 68

Section 8. During play time—moving from one activity to another

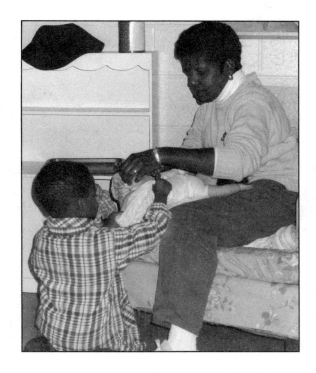

Ages two-and-a-half through four-and-a-half:

Moving from one activity to another, over the days and weeks, the children respond intently to fresh materials and to ideas coming from each other and from their teachers.

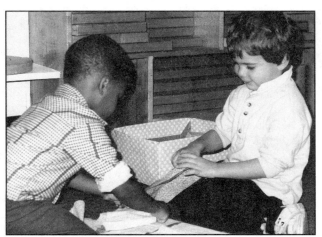

"If recent research is beginning to clarify the ways children benefit from play, it is also clarifying the ways adults can enhance play." Curriculum Planning, p. 26

Section 8. During play time—playing "house"

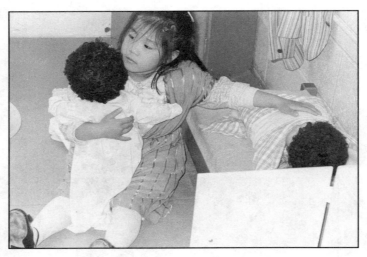

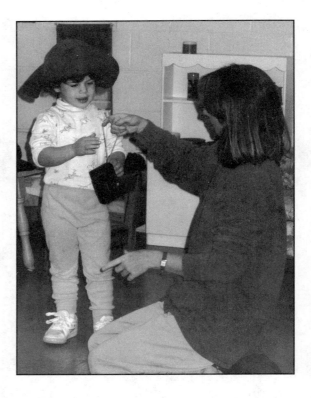

These future mothers, job-holders, and community participants appear to be trying out roles they have observed. Their abilities to nurture, to develop skills, and to take on the world may already be apparent.

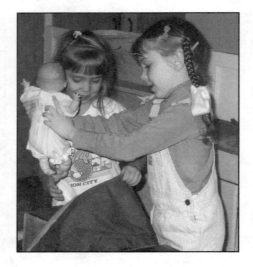

"Each child is viewed as a unique person with an individual pattern and timing of growth and development. The curriculum and adults' interaction are responsive to individual differences in ability and interests." DAP, p. 54

Section 8. During play time—playing "house"

How clear it is that children learn by imitating adults!

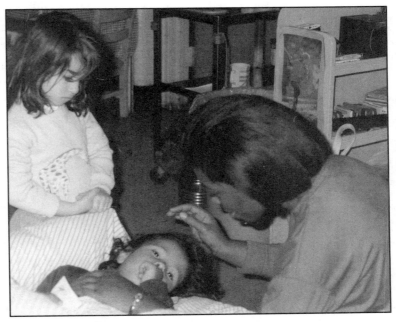

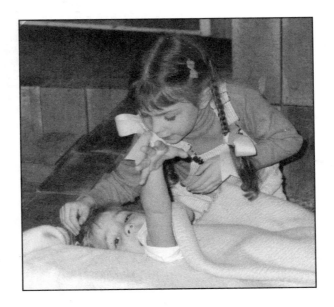

"Pretend play seems to be an important activity for young children. [R]esearch...document[s] its contribution to children's social and cognitive development." Curriculum Planning, p. 27

Section 8. During play time—building with blocks

This is how quality education looks as children engage in thought about shape, balance, weight, height. They enjoy their interactions with the blocks, with each other, and with their teachers.

"Learning about math, science, social studies, health, and other content areas are all integrated through meaningful activities such as those when children build with blocks." DAP, p. 56

Section 8. During play time—building with blocks

What does the teacher do during free play? He or she

- encourages
- guides
- helps
- adds materials
- keeps the peace
- observes and plans
- stays "in there"...
  tuned in
  attentive
  interested
  supportive

This five-and-a-half-year-old boy thinks about shape and design as he constructs; then when he has finished, he writes his name to tape to his building.

Call his accomplishment an avenue to self-esteem;
Call it creativity;
Call it problem solving;
Call it diligence, concentration;
Call it play.

"...symbolic play is influenced by the play materials available to the child. In young children, play is enhanced by realistic materials and realistic toy props." Curriculum Planning, p. 23

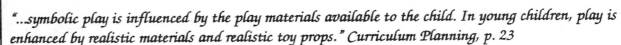

27

Section 9. Teachers alert to children's appearance, behavior

Roberto, usually so busily involved and friendly, seems not himself today, even though he tries to occupy himself.

Teachers, aides, and volunteers stay alert, try not to miss a beat—checking when a child's appearance or manner changes, when there are signs of tension, fatigue, or malaise.

"Adults are aware of the symptoms of common illnesses, alert to changes in children's behavior that may signal illness or allergies." DAP, p. 45

Section 9. Teachers alert to children's appearance, behavior

It helps parents enormously to know that teachers are mindful of their children's well-being...

helping...
listening...
consoling...
strengthening...
planning.

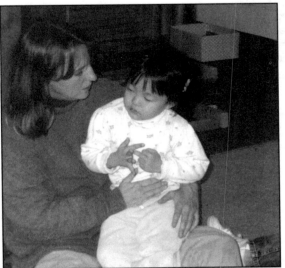

"As children work with materials or activities, teachers listen, observe, and interpret children's behavior." DAP, p. 5

Section 9. Observing and recording

Good teachers <u>observe</u>—along with everything else they do—making it a point to jot down notes of their observations whenever possible and to confer with each other during quieter moments of the day.

"Appropriate curriculum planning is based on teachers' observations and recordings of each child's special interests and developmental progress." DAP, p. 3

Section 9. Observing and recording

Teachers learn how easy it is to forget details of all that happens, so they try to jot down notes about the children whenever they can during quiet moments at the center—in and out of doors and during and after school hours. Record-keeping (when teachers have only a few extra seconds) consists of brief notes about individual children or the program; about very successful or stressful events; about injury or health issues; about family matters of concern to children or staff; about any subject which bears on a child's education and well-being. Then, on their own time, teachers fill in the details and organize all of their notes for future use.

"Developmental assessment of children's progress and achievement is used to plan curriculum, identify children with special needs, communicate with parents, and evaluate the program's effectiveness." DAP, p. 57

Section 10. Discipline

But no matter how well-trained a teacher may be, no matter how well she or he has prepared the curriculum, arranged wonderful materials, and supervised and guided the children—disciplinary problems and solutions are always at the core of life with children.

This small boy, Mike, finds himself engaged in a dispute...then "explaining" to his teacher.

"Staff use positive techniques of guidance, including redirection, anticipation of and elimination of potential problems, positive reinforcement, and encouragement rather than competition, comparison, or criticism. Staff abstain from corporal punishment or other humiliating or frightening discipline techniques. Consistent, clear rules are explained to children and understood by adults." Accreditation, p. 9

Section 10. Discipline

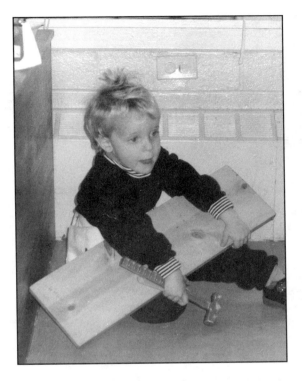

Now he tries a new idea with his board (which he likes to carry around with a set of play tools). He approaches Rudi, and another argument begins. More teacher intervention takes place, with her attempts to hear him out and to go over the rules with him. Mike, just turned three, is new to the program.

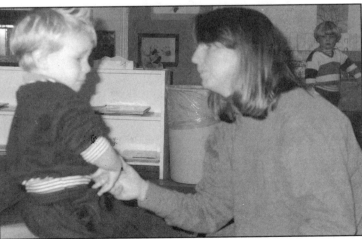

The teacher seems firm, unflappable; she is a good listener, and she is fair, and comfortable about being in charge. But the "right" solution is hard to come by this morning.

"GOAL: The program is staffed by adults who understand child development and who recognize and provide for children's needs."
Accreditation, p. 18

33

Section 10. Discipline

Even in the best programs, discipline problems are part of life—more on some days than others. Successful teachers help children learn how to go about settling difficulties on their own, but the teachers know that is a gradual process, and they stop children from hurting each other.

Once again Mike is at the center of a dispute, first with Brandon, then with Tony.

The teacher knows that a firm, direct response would be effective with children a little older and more experienced; however, right now with this very young boy, she decides on diversion. It's off to the kitchen. "Let's see what the cook is fixing for lunch in that big pot. Yes, you may have a turn stirring." She views this diversion not as rewarding him but rather as a way to give him some respite from her vigilant work with him. He needs time and relaxation in order to integrate all that is happening to him.

She is prepared to take time, here at the center, to help start him on the long road leading to self-discipline.

"Teachers facilitate the development of self-control in children by using positive guidance techniques such as modeling and encouraging expected behavior, redirecting children to a more acceptable activity, and setting clear limits." DAP, p. 55

Section 10. Discipline

Now that the teacher has helped Mike settle down with a puzzle, Brandon bursts into angry tears. Indeed, it is one of those days. The teacher hears Brandon out, decides to involve him in another activity (he's not interested) or another friend (he _is_ interested) and this works, with the staying power of her continuing presence. This teacher's experience and knowledge tell her that in such a disciplinary situation as this, her job is not merely to correct misbehavior but to educate children in ways to manage their relationships.

"Limits are set for children but the environment is arranged so that a minimal number of no's are necessary, particularly for very young children." Accreditation, p. 9

Section 10. Discipline

Learning to become self-disciplined takes children—and adults—a long time.

On another day, we have Paulette and Arabella...

Arabella grabs Paulette's toy.

Paulette: "TEACHER!"

"Adults respond quickly and directly to children's needs, desires, and messages and adapt their responses to children's differing styles and abilities." DAP, p. 9

Section 10. Discipline

The teacher gets there fast—calling first for her assistant to take over for a few minutes. Then she is free to listen to Arabella and Paulette in turn, and to comfort them, to go over rules, to help them talk out their feelings, and think of a different way next time.

"Adult behaviors that are <u>never</u> acceptable toward children include: screaming in anger; neglect; inflicting physical or emotional pain; criticism of a child's person or family by ridiculing, blaming, teasing, insulting, name-calling, threatening, or using frightening or humiliating punishment....Children learn self-control when adults treat them with dignity and use discipline techniques such as guiding...valuing mistakes as learning opportunities...redirecting...listening when children talk about their feelings and frustrations...reminding children of rules...." DAP, p. 11

Section 10. Discipline

On still another day: Problem here?....

I'm going to stop you from kicking, Lars....

Tony, stop! <u>Tell</u> Lars. Tell him with your words.

Lars, listen to Tony.

We're going to work this out.

Zak, tell <u>her</u> what you're telling me....

Tell her how you feel.

"Children's verbalization of emotions and ideas is both a goal for and an indicator of a good quality program. While preverbal children will naturally communicate physically, staff members redirect their actions constructively and encourage verbal expression." Accreditation, p. 10

Section 10. Discipline

Vaughn, can you tell me what's the matter? I am listening to you. Please don't yell at me—I can't help you when you yell. Use your words...tell me.

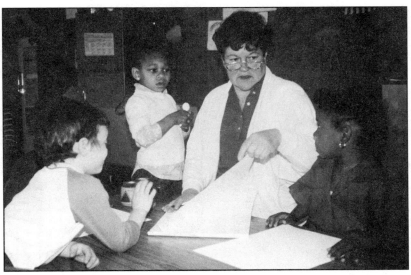

To recapitulate: children learn from teachers who are:

warm, understanding;

tuned in;

fair;

genuine;

good-humored;

good listeners.

"Children's communication skills develop from verbal interaction with adults." Accreditation, p. 9

39

Section 11. Language in a print-rich environment

Words are necessary for much more than disputes and momentary crises. In print-rich environments, children see words—fresh, changing words—all around them...most on child's-eye-level. The children become immersed in language.

Christopher and Brian S. at work in their office

Lindsay is busy cutting with scissors.

...and Amy with their pattern block designs

Haruka with her pattern block design

Christopher with his pattern block wall.

Children marching in a parade around the room.

Apple Prints

"...[p]roviding a print-rich environment...stimulates the development of language and literacy skills in a meaningful context."
DAP, p. 6

Section 11. Language in a print-rich environment

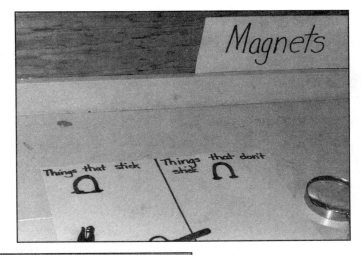

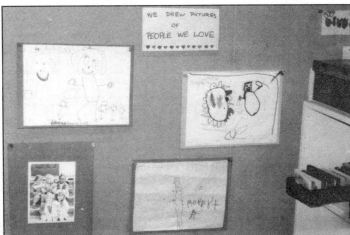

"Label things in room, use written words with pictures and spoken language." Accreditation, p. 41

Section 11. Language in a print-rich environment

"Learning to read is largely a matter of coming to know about written language. In order for children to construct knowledge about written language, they must be provided meaningful print with which to interact....It is just something else to explore and to learn about, right along with the blocks and the paint." *Curriculum Planning, pp. 76-77*

Section 11. Language in print-rich environment

Five-year-old Daniel has served the meal and enjoys sitting next to "big" Daniel (a student-observer) and sharing first names.

(Many student-teachers and observers add energy, knowledge, fresh ideas, and important insight and assistance to programs which are able to include them.)

"Meal times need to be pleasant activities in which conversation is encouraged and independence fostered. Adults should interact with children during meals..." Accreditation, p. 36

Section 12. Out of doors—more communication

Talking and listening—using language—go on all through the day in all spaces, both in and out of doors. Children and teachers communicate, sharing special thoughts, projects, and skills.

"Because their physical development is occurring so rapidly, young children through age 8 need daily outdoor experiences to practice large muscle skills, learn about outdoor environments, and experience freedom not always possible indoors. <u>Outdoor time is an integral part of the curriculum</u> and requires planning; it is not simply a time for children to release pent-up energy." (emphasis added) DAP, p. 8

Section 12. Outdoor curriculum

These teachers don't distance themselves from the children on the playground any more than they would indoors. They stay connected to the children, their activities, their fantasy play...

Teachers enrich outdoor play with simple, noncommercial playthings like tree trunks, jump ropes, soapy bubbles and straws....

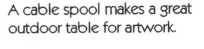

A cable spool makes a great outdoor table for artwork.

"There is little argument that playgrounds created by adults and children working together are more stimulating and developmentally appropriate than conventional ones." Curriculum Planning, p. 55

Section 12. Outdoor curriculum

These teachers constantly think of ways to make the curriculum in their "outdoor classrooms" as enjoyable and educational as the indoors.

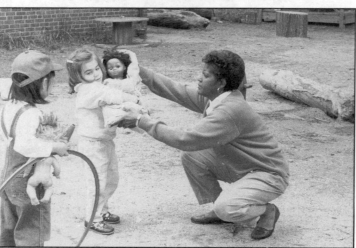

"...children vary in their levels of development. In terms of outdoor play, this means that children will have different climbing abilities, running skills, balancing skills, coordination, and strength. The play environment then is equipped and arranged to present graduated challenges appropriate to the skills of all children playing there. In addition, the equipment should be sufficiently varied to allow children to engage in all of the cognitive forms of play (exercise, dramatic, construction, and games with rules), to develop social skills through interaction with peers, and to allow for quiet solitude and reflection." Curriculum Planning, p. 54

Section 12. Transition to indoors

Transition comes now, from outdoors to cubbies in the hallway or class-room. Some children ask for help; some help each other. A few don't need any help—each is on his or her own unique developmental timetable.

"Routines are tailored to children's needs and rhythms as much as possible." Accreditation, p. 42

Section 13. Self-help and adult help during routines

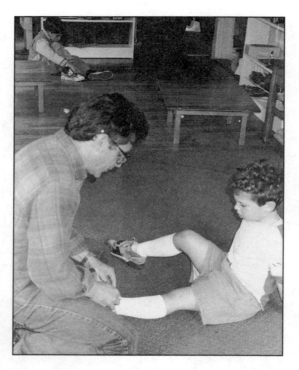

There's an art to knowing which children truly need a hand when they ask for help, which ones could use help and won't ask, and which ones need a gentle challenge.

"Adults watch to see what the child is trying to do and provide the necessary support to help the child accomplish the task, allowing children to do what they are capable of doing and assisting with tasks that are frustrating." DAP, p. 40

Section 13. Self-help and adult help during routines

Chores before lunch: Morale looks good here as the children clean up and prepare for what comes next in the day. The room is the children's own special place, and each one participates in the responsibility of caring for it.

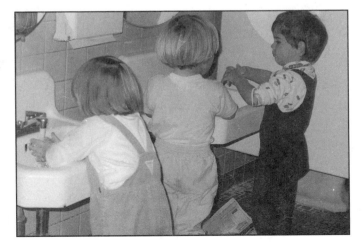

"Basic learning materials and activities for an appropriate curriculum include...classroom responsibilities, such as helping with routines, and positive interactions and problem-solving opportunities with other children and adults." DAP, p. 4

Section 14. Lunch

Time for a sit-down, family-style lunch. Whether the food comes from home, packed in lunch boxes, or is prepared by the cook in the center's kitchen, the goal is for children and adults to eat together in a relaxed, friendly, conversational manner—enjoying favorite tastes and learning new ones, taking their time, and feeling companionable during this shared part of the day.

"Family-style meals allow children to take as many spoonfuls of a food as needed. Children can dish out a second portion without adult help if bowls of food are available at the table." Curriculum Planning, p. 18

Section 14. Lunch

Young children do best when adults sit down with them at mealtime...the teacher, a volunteer, sometimes a mother or father who has dropped in for lunch, to everyone's delight.

"Meals and snacktimes are pleasant social and learning experiences for children. Foods indicative of children's cultural backgrounds are served periodically. At least one adult sits with children during meals." Accreditation, p. 36

Section 15. Cleanup—time for nap

Responsible cleanup after lunch is one of the finishing touches before nap/rest time.

Teachers who are committed to an afternoon nap for preschool children are most often successful in managing naps. Of course it takes many children awhile to settle down; nonetheless, most finally do. Even kindergartners in some centers go down for a rest on their mats—and some fall asleep.

"Adults need to think carefully about how activities are sequenced. Are there enough alternations of quiet time with more active times?" Curriculum Planning, p. 16

Section 16. During nap

Sometimes (not always) it's possible for teachers to catch up on informal conferencing, note-taking, and working together on materials—and, one hopes, to get off their feet for a brief respite.

It's also a time when some teachers end their shifts and new staff takes over, bringing each other up to date on what has been happening.

"Regular communication and understanding about child development form a basis for mutual problem solving about concerns regarding behavior and growth." DAP, p. 12

Section 16. After nap

A sleepy feeling often prevails after nap. An afternoon snack helps, and hearing the teacher read another story-book.

"Children can feel free to learn and try different activities if they feel loved or cared for by adults." Curriculum Planning, p. 19

Section 16. After nap

Millions of young children spend long hours at children's centers or in family child care programs. It's a challenge to teachers to provide a rich and ever-interesting program.

These teachers try to come up with fresh ideas for late afternoon activities: cooking, sometimes; an occasional sewing project (this time making small pillows); and one day seeing how to mix a new color—lavender—with paint, and then trying it at the easel.

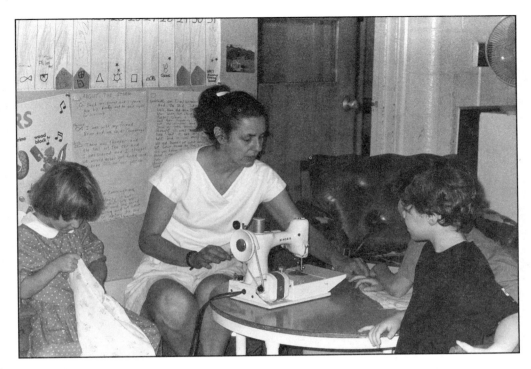

"Interactions and activities are designed to develop children's self-esteem and positive feelings toward learning."
DAP, p. 53

55

Section 16. After nap

There aren't always special projects. On more ordinary days, free play is taken up again during late afternoon hours—more ambitious activities for the kindergartners, and more freewheeling ones for threes and fours.

"Teachers can use child development knowledge to identify the range of appropriate behaviors, activities, and materials for a specific age group...Children's play is a primary vehicle for and indicator of their mental growth." DAP, pp. 2-3

Section 17. Late in the afternoon

These four-year-olds are dressed to go home at the end of the day, and one has just spotted her mother.

If parent and teacher need to talk about a child at pick-up time, they move off to one side, out of the child's hearing.

Although late afternoon teachers can't leave the children for very long to talk with parents coming to pick up their children, they do try to chat briefly about how the day has gone. Longer exchanges wait until evening or weekend telephoning or conferencing.

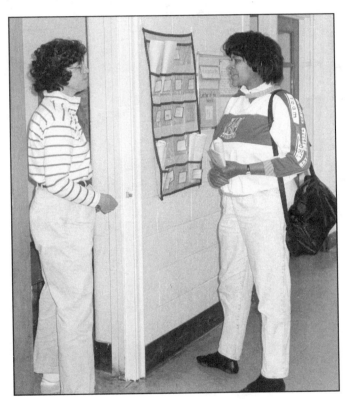

"...early childhood teachers must work in partnership with families and communicate regularly with children's parents...children are largely dependent on their families for identity, security, care, and a general sense of well-being."
DAP, p. 12

Section 17. Early evening

It may seem like a long day for those children whose parents can't arrive to get them until closing time.

"The pace of the program day will vary depending on the length of time children are present...." DAP, p. 8

Some final thoughts, hopes, and observations

59

Section 18. Conclusion

Excellent teachers have studied subjects like child development, but they never stop trying to learn more. They know growth patterns. They accept the fear, pain, and aggression in children's primitive behavior— and help with ways to cope. They set forth firm limits and offer guidance. They believe in the forward momentum of growth—that children <u>will</u> learn and mature, in time. Finally, they are willing to improvise and to make good use of intuition and insight.

Master teachers are only human; they too have awful, discouraging days when they need help and counsel on the spot. Much of the time, though, as we watch them moving effectively through unexpected events as well as classroom routines, we know that their quality cannot come simply from their knowledge or their advance preparation. Teacher-training "Methods" courses prepare teachers for much of their work: developing a dynamic curriculum, say, or generating parent programs, or promoting sound nutrition for children and families. But no methods, no recipes, can forecast children's spontaneous behavior and give teachers an advance script for what to do or say when the unforeseen occurs, when sad or maddening or wildly funny or confusing things happen, or when children fasten onto ideas or projects of their own that bear no resemblance to the teachers' plans.

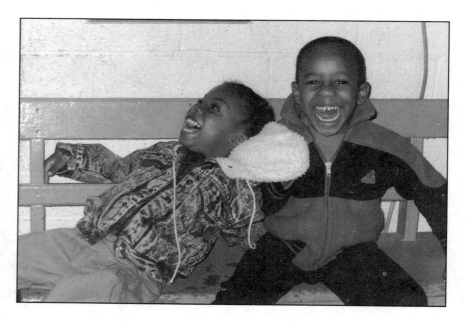

Section 18. Conclusion

Our children look to us to teach them, guide them, and befriend them. We look to ourselves to do our very best for them.

How do master teachers function so well in this complex and often unpredictable world of preschool education? One possible answer is that they demonstrate a commitment to the <u>art</u> (as well as science) of teaching:

...being constantly attentive to children's faces, voices, bodies, behaviors

...planning what to do for children—and <u>with</u> them—that will be fun, fascinating, educational, and also safe and comfortable

...listening, observing, reflecting; and then responding—teaching from the very <u>core</u> of their knowledge, with respect, with nurturing, and with a flair for challenge—not too little nor too much; just the right, sensitive match

...communicating openly with children, families, colleagues

* * * * * * * * * * * * * *

For further reading

Baker, K. R. (1966). <u>Let's play outdoors.</u> Washington, DC: NAEYC.

Bredekamp, S. (Ed.). (1987). <u>Developmentally appropriate practice in early childhood programs serving children from birth through age 8.</u> Washington, DC: NAEYC.

Brown, J. F. (Ed.). (1982). <u>Curriculum planning for young children.</u> Washington, DC: NAEYC.

Derman-Sparks, L. (1989). <u>Anti-bias curriculum: Tools for empowering young children.</u> Washington, DC: NAEYC.

Hill, D. M. (1977). <u>Mud, sand, and water.</u> Washington, DC: NAEYC.

Hirsch, E. S. (Ed.). (1984). <u>The block book</u> (rev. ed.). Washington, DC: NAEYC.

Holt, B. (1989). <u>Science with young children</u> (rev. ed.). Washington, DC: NAEYC.

Jalongo, M. R. (1988). <u>Young children and picture books: Literature from infancy to six.</u> Washington, DC: NAEYC.

Jervis, K. (Ed.). (1984). <u>Separation: Strategies for helping two to four-year-olds.</u> Washington, DC: NAEYC.

Lasky, L., & Mukerji, R. (1980). <u>Art: Basic for young children.</u> Washington, DC: NAEYC.

McDonald, D. T. (1979). <u>Music in our lives: The early years.</u> Washington, DC: NAEYC.

Riley, S. S. (1984). <u>How to generate values in young children: Integrity, honesty, individuality, self-confidence, and wisdom.</u> Washington, DC: NAEYC.

Sawyers, J. K., & Rogers, C. S. (1988). <u>Helping young children develop through play: A practical guide for parents, caregivers, and teachers.</u> Washington, DC: NAEYC.

Stone, J. G. (1969). <u>A guide to discipline.</u> Washington, DC: NAEYC.

Stone, J. G. (1987). <u>Teacher-parent relationships.</u> Washington, DC: NAEYC.

Sullivan, M. (1982). <u>Feeling strong, feeling free: Movement exploration for young children.</u> Washington, DC: NAEYC.

Warren, R. M. (1977). <u>Caring: Supporting children's growth.</u> Washington, DC: NAEYC.

Zavitkovsky, D., Baker, K. R., Berlfein, J. R., & Almy, M. (1986). <u>Listen to the children.</u> Washington, DC: NAEYC.

Information About NAEYC

NAEYC is...

...a membership-supported organization of people committed to fostering the growth and development of children from birth through age eight. Membership is open to all who share a desire to serve and act on behalf of the needs and rights of young children.

NAEYC provides...

...educational services and resources to adults who work with and for children, including

- **Young Children,** the journal for early childhood educators
- Books, posters, brochures, and videos to expand your knowledge and commitment to young children, with topics including infants, curriculum, research, discipline, teacher education, and parent involvement
- An **Annual Conference** that brings people from all over the country to share their expertise and advocate on behalf of children and families
- **Week of the Young Child** celebrations sponsored by NAEYC Affiliate Groups across the nation to call public attention to the needs and rights of children and families
- Insurance plans for individuals and programs
- **Public affairs** information for knowledgeable advocacy efforts at all levels of government and through the media
- The **National Academy of Early Childhood Programs,** a voluntary accreditation system for high-quality programs for children
- The **Information Service,** a centralized source of information-sharing, distribution, and collaboration

For free information about membership, publications, or other NAEYC services...
...call NAEYC at 202-232-8777 or 800-424-2460 or write to NAEYC, 1834 Connecticut Ave., N.W., Washington, DC 20009-5786.